CHILD'S BIBLE HISTORY

CHILD'S BIBLE HISTORY

—BY THE—

MOST REV. F. J. KNECHT, D.D.

TAN BOOKS AND PUBLISHERS, INC.
Rockford, Illinois 61105

NIHIL OBSTAT:
F. J. Holweck
Censor Librorum, Sti. Ludovici
die 15, Maii, 1940

IMPRIMATUR:
Joannes J. Glennon
Archiepiscopus, Sti. Ludovici
die 16, Maii, 1940

Originally published by B. Herder Book Co.

PRINTED AND BOUND IN THE UNITED STATES OF AMERICA

TAN BOOKS AND PUBLISHERS, INC.
P.O. Box 424
Rockford, Illinois 61105

1973

CONTENTS

FIRST PART

HISTORY OF THE OLD TESTAMENT

SECOND PART

HISTORY OF THE NEW TESTAMENT

Chapter *Page*

FIRST PART

HISTORY OF THE OLD TESTAMENT

---

1. The Creation of the World

IN THE beginning God created heaven and earth. But the earth was dark and empty. And God said: "Let there be light." And there was light. This was the first day.

On the second day God said: "Let there be a firmament." And it was so done. God called the firmament Heaven.

2. On the third day God said: "Let the waters of the Earth be gathered together in one place, and let the dry land appear." And it was so done. God called the dry land Earth, and the gathering of the waters He called Sea.

God said again: "Let the earth bring forth grass, herbs and fruit trees." And it was so done. The earth was covered with grass, and herbs, and trees yielding fruit.

3. On the fourth day God said: "Let there be lights in the firmament." And it was so done. God created the sun, the moon and the stars, to rule the day and the night, and to divide the light from the darkness.

On the fifth day God said: "Let there be fishes in the water and birds in the air." And God created the fishes and the birds, according to their kinds.

THE CREATION OF THE WORLD

4. On the sixth day God said: "Let the earth bring forth cattle and beasts of every kind." And it was so done. And God created the beasts and the cattle, and every creature that creeps on the earth. Lastly, God created man.

On the seventh day God rested, and He blessed that day and made it holy.

QUESTIONS

1. What did God create in the beginning? How was the earth? What did God say and create on the first day? On the second? 2. What did God say and create on the third day? What did God say again? 3, 4. What did God say and create on the fourth, the fifth and the sixth days? What did God do on the seventh day?

2. The Creation and the Fall of the Angels

BESIDES the visible world, God created also an invisible world, namely, the angels of heaven. At first they were all good and happy.

2. But many angels became proud, and would no longer be obedient to God. Then Michael and the other good angels fought against the wicked spirits. The bad angels were conquered, and cast from heaven down to hell. The leader of the fallen angels was Lucifer. He is also called Satan or the Devil.

3. God rewarded the good angels by giving them eternal happiness.

QUESTIONS

1. What did God create besides the visible world? 2. Who fought against the bad angels? 3. How did God reward the good angels?

3. The Creation of the First Man—Paradise

WHEN God created man, He formed a human body of the slime of the earth, breathed into his face the breath of life, and man became a living being. God called him Adam, which means, man taken from the earth.

2. The Lord made, expressly for man, a beautiful garden, called Paradise. There were in it all sorts of trees, and all kinds of delicious fruits. God placed Adam in this garden, and said to him: "Of every tree of Paradise thou mayest eat. But thou shalt not eat of the tree which is in the midst of the garden. For if thou eatest of it, thou shalt die the death."

3. As yet Adam was the only man. Therefore, God caused Adam to fall into a deep sleep, and then took one of his ribs and formed of it a woman. When Adam awoke, God brought the woman to him. Adam was pleased, and called the woman Eve, which means Mother of the Living.

4. Adam and Eve lived quite happily in Paradise. They were perfect and just, and knew nothing of wickedness.

QUESTIONS

1. How did God form the body of the first man? 2. Where did God place Adam? Of what tree was Adam forbidden to eat? 3. In what manner was Eve created? 4. How did Adam and Eve live in Paradise?

4. The Fall of Our First Parents

THE devil looked with envy on the happiness of Adam and Eve. To deceive them, he made use of the serpent. The serpent said to Eve: "Why has God commanded you not to eat of every tree of Paradise?"

2. Eve answered: "We do eat of the trees of the garden. But God has commanded us not to eat of the tree which stands in the midst of Paradise, lest we die."

3. The serpent replied: "No, surely you shall not die if you eat of it. On the contrary, your eyes shall be opened, and you shall be like God." Eve gave way to pride, she looked at the fruit, and saw that it was beautiful and good. She took and ate of it. Then she gave to Adam, and he also did eat. Thus was the first sin committed.

4. Now their eyes were opened, and they saw that they were naked. Filled with shame, they began to sew together fig leaves to cover their nakedness. But soon they heard the voice of God, and they hid themselves among the trees of the garden. Then God called and said: "Adam, where art thou?"

5. Adam answered: "I am afraid, for I am naked, and have hidden myself."

God said: "Who told thee that thou art naked; but that thou hast eaten of the forbidden fruit?"

Adam answered: "The woman gave me of it, and I did eat."

Then the Lord asked the woman: "Why hast thou done this?"

She replied: "The serpent deceived me, and I did eat."

QUESTIONS

1. Of whom did the devil make use to deceive our first parents? 2. What did Eve reply? 3. What did Eve do when the serpent said that their eyes would be opened? 4. Why did they hide, when God came to call them? 5. What did God say to Adam and Eve, and what did they answer?

5. The Punishment of Our First Parents—The Promise of a Savior

THEN the Lord said to the serpent: "Because thou hast done this, thou art cursed among all the beasts of the earth. I will put enmity between thee and the woman, thy seed and her seed. She shall crush thy head." This refers to the Savior.

THE FALL OF OUR FIRST PARENTS

2. To Eve he said: "Thou shalt have great sorrow with thy children, and thou shalt be under the control of thy husband."

3. To Adam the Lord said: "Cursed be the earth in thy work. Thorns and thistles shall it bring forth to thee. In the sweat of thy face thou shalt eat thy bread, till thou shalt return to the earth, out of which thou wast taken: For dust thou art, and unto dust thou shalt return."

4. Then God made garments of skins for Adam and his wife. Hereupon he drove them out of Paradise.

QUESTIONS

1. How did God curse the serpent? 2. How did God punish Eve? 3. What did He say to Adam? 4. What garments did God make for Adam and Eve?

6. Cain and Abel

ADAM and Eve had two sons. The elder was called Cain, the younger Abel. Cain became a husbandman, Abel a shepherd. Abel was just; but Cain was wicked.

2. One day they offered a sacrifice to God. Cain offered the fruits of the earth, Abel sacrificed the firstlings of his flock. God looked with pleasure on Abel and on his gifts; but upon Cain and his offerings He looked not. Then Cain grew very angry, and his countenance became dark and sullen.

3. The Lord said to Cain: "Why art thou angry? And why is thy countenance fallen? If thou do well, thou shalt be rewarded; but if thou do ill, punishment shall forthwith be present at the door: Keep away from sin."

DEATH OF ABEL

4. Cain, however, did not hearken to the Lord. One day he said to his brother: "Come, let us go forth into the fields." And when they were there, Cain rose up against his brother Abel, and slew him.

5. The Lord asked Cain: "Where is thy brother Abel?" Cain answered: "I know not; am I my brother's keeper?"

God said to him: "What hast thou done? The voice of thy brother's blood crieth to Me from the earth. Therefore, cursed shalt thou be upon the earth. When thou shalt till it, it shall not yield to thee its fruit. A fugitive and a vagabond shalt thou be upon the earth."

6. Thereupon Cain went out from the face of the Lord, and dwelt as a fugitive on the earth.

QUESTIONS

1. How were the two sons of Adam and Eve called? 2. What did they offer to God one day? 3. What did the Lord say to Cain who was angry? 4. How did Cain kill Abel? 5. What did the Lord say to Cain, and how did He punish him? 6. How did Cain dwell upon the earth?

7. The Building of the Ark

ADAM and Eve had many sons and daughters. The number of men increased continually. But sin and crime kept on multiplying in the same manner.

God said: "I will destroy man from the face of the earth."

2. In the midst of that wicked generation there was one just and virtuous man, called Noe. God said to him: "Make thee an ark of timber planks, and pitch it within and without. Thou shalt make

a window in the ark, and a door in its side. Behold! I will send heavy rains upon the earth. All things that are on the earth shall perish. But thou and thy family shall go into the ark. Take with thee a pair of every sort of beasts, and food for thee and the beasts."

3. Noe did all things as God had commanded. He spent a hundred years in building the ark, and never ceased to preach penance to the people.

4. But they heeded not the warning; they ate, and drank, and held great feasts.

QUESTIONS

1. What was multiplied on earth as the number of men increased? 2. Who was Noe? What did God tell him to do? 3. How many years did Noe spend in building the ark? 4. Did the people heed his warning?

8. The Deluge

THE Lord spoke to Noe: "Go into the ark. I shall send rain for forty days and forty nights. All living creatures shall be destroyed from the face of the earth."

2. Noe went into the ark. With him went his wife, his three sons and the wives of his sons, and the beasts. The Lord himself shut the ark from the outside.

3. Then the great fountains of the deep were broken up, and the flood-gates of heaven were opened, and the rain fell upon the earth for forty days and forty nights. The waters continued to increase, and lifted the ark from the earth. The flood rose fifteen cubits above the highest mountains. But the ark floated upon the surging waters.

THE DELUGE

4. Thus was destroyed every creature that lived on the earth, from man to beast, from the bird in the air to the worm under the earth. Noe alone was spared, and those that were with him in the ark.

QUESTIONS

1. What did the Lord say to Noe? 2. Who went with Noe into the ark? 3. What happened during forty days and forty nights? 4. What was thus destroyed, and who alone remained?

9. Noe's Offering—The Rainbow

THE waters remained one hundred and fifty days on the earth. Then God sent a warm wind on the earth. The waters abated by little and little, and the ark rested on a high mountain in Armenia.

NOE'S OFFERING

2. When the earth was completely dry, God said to Noe: "Go out of the ark with thy family, and with all the beasts."

3. Noe did so, taking with him his family and all the beasts. Filled with gratitude, he built an altar and offered a sacrifice to the Lord. God was pleased with the sacrifice. He made a rainbow in the sky, and said: "Never again will I destroy mankind by a flood. The rainbow in the clouds shall be the sign of my covenant with the earth."

QUESTIONS

1. What did God send after one hundred and fifty days? 2. What happened when the earth was completely dry? 3. What did Noe offer on leaving the ark? What did God do and say?

10. The Call of Abraham

THE descendants of Noe soon multiplied. But as they grew in numbers so they increased in wickedness. Men no longer adored the one true God, but instead of their Creator, they worshiped living creatures, and even lifeless pictures.

2. At that time there lived in the land of Chaldea a virtuous man, called Abraham. It was to him that God said: "Go forth out of thy own country to the land which I will show thee. I will make thee the father of a great nation, and I will bless thee."

3. Abraham believed God, and set out for Chanaan. There the Lord appeared to him a second time and said: "Behold! I will give this land to thee and to thy posterity."

4. Thenceforth Chanaan was called the Promised Land, because God had promised it to Abraham and to his descendants.

5. Afterwards the Lord appeared again to Abraham and said: "I will make a covenant with thee: I will be with thee and with thy posterity. But ye shall obey Me. I am your Lord and Master. This is the sign of My covenant with you: Among you every male child shall be circumcised on the eighth day after his birth."

6. Abraham was then ninety-nine years old, and had no children. God said to him: "After a year Sara, thy wife, shall have a son."

QUESTIONS

1. What did the descendants of Noe adore instead of the one true God? 2. What did God say to Abraham? 3. What did Abraham do? 4. How was Chanaan henceforth called. 5. What covenant did the Lord make with Abraham? 6. What did God promise to Abraham when he was ninety-nine of age?

11. The Sacrifice of Abraham

SARA gave birth to a child as the Lord had promised. Abraham, who was then a hundred years old, called his son Isaac, and circumcised him on the eighth day.

2. When the boy was grown, God tried Abraham. One night the Lord said to him: "Abraham, take thy only begotten son Isaac, whom thou lovest, and go to Mount Moria, and there sacrifice him to Me for a holocaust."

3. Early in the morning Abraham arose, and cut the wood for the sacrifice. The wood he laid upon the shoulders of Isaac; he himself carried fire and a sword.

As they went along, Issac said: "My father?"

Abraham answered: "What wilt thou, my son?"

Isaac exclaimed: "Behold! here is fire and wood, but where is the victim for the holocaust?"

Abraham replied: "God will provide Himself a victim, my son."

4. Thus they went on together. On the top of the mount Abraham erected an altar, placed the wood upon it, bound his son and laid him on the wood. Then Abraham put forth his hand, and took the sword to sacrifice his son. But lo! an angel from heaven cried out to him, saying: "Lay not thy hand upon the boy. For now I know thou fearest God, and hast not spared thy only begotten son, for My sake."

5. Then Abraham lifted up his eyes, and saw a ram sticking fast by the horns in the briers. He took the ram and offered him for a holocaust, instead of his son.

6. The angel of the Lord spoke again to Abra-

ABRAHAM'S SACRIFICE

ham: "Thus speaketh the Lord: Because thou hast done this thing, and hast not spared thy only begotten son, I will bless thee and multiply thy seeds as the stars of heaven, and as the sand that is by the sea-shore. And in thy seed all the nations of the earth shall be blessed." The last words refer to the Savior.

7. Abraham then returned home with his son. Isaac, carrying the wood, is a figure of Christ, carrying His cross.

QUESTIONS

1. How old was Abraham when Isaac was born? 2. What did God say to Abraham when Isaac was grown up? 3. What did Abraham do? What did Isaac ask? 4. What did Abraham erect when they came to the mountain? What did the angel cry out? 5. What was sticking in the briers? 6. What did the angel of the Lord speak again? 7. Of whom was Isaac a figure?

12. Joseph is Hated by His Brothers

NOW, after these things, it came to pass that Isaac also had a son, whom he called Jacob. But Jacob had twelve sons, and he loved Joseph above all the others, because he was young and very good. And Jacob made him a beautiful coat of divers colors. One day the brothers of Joseph were all tending their flocks, and some of them committed a most wicked crime. Joseph was very sorry, and told his father what had happened. On this account his brothers hated him, and would not speak to him kindly.

2. It also happened that Joseph had a wonderful dream. He said to his brothers: "Hear my dream: I thought we were binding sheaves in the field. My sheaf arose and stood upright; your sheaves, however, standing around, bowed down before my sheaf."

3. Whereup his brothers exclaimed: "Shalt thou be our king?" And they hated him more than ever.

QUESTIONS

1. Who was the son of Isaac? Why was Joseph hated by his brothers? 2. What did Joseph dream about his sheaf and the sheaves of his brothers? 3. What did his brothers exclaim?

13. Joseph is Sold by His Brothers

ONE day the sons of Jacob had gone with their flocks to Sichem. Jacob said to Joseph: "Go and see, if all be well with thy brothers and the cattle." Joseph obeyed, and went to see them.

JOSEPH SOLD BY HIS BROTHERS

2. When his brothers saw him afar off, they exclaimed: "Here comes the dreamer; let us kill him, and say that some wild beast has devoured him."

3. As soon as Joseph drew near to his brothers, they stripped him of his coat of divers colors, and cast him into an old pit. Then they sat down to eat. Meanwhile they beheld merchants passing by, with camels carrying spices, balm and myrrh into Egypt.

4. Juda then said to his brothers: "What does it profit us to kill our brother? It is better that he be sold to these merchants, and that our hands be not defiled; for he is our brother."

5. The others agreed, drew Joseph out of the pit, and sold him for twenty pieces of silver. Joseph wept and besought his brothers, but in vain. The merchants led him away with them to Egypt.

6. Jacob knew not what had become of his son. He cried: "A wild beast hath devoured Joseph." He mourned a long time, and would not be comforted.

Joseph, sold by his brothers, is a figure of Christ, sold by Judas.

QUESTIONS

1. What did Jacob one day say to Joseph? 2. What did the brothers say when they saw Joseph coming? 3. What did they do to him? 4. What did Juda say? 5. For how much did they sell Joseph? 6. What did Jacob cry out?

14. Joseph in the House of Putiphar

ON arriving in Egypt the merchants sold Joseph to Putiphar, the captain of the Royal Guard. The Lord was with Joseph, and blessed him in all his undertakings. And Putiphar loved Joseph, and gave him charge over all his household.

2. Now the wife of Putiphar was very wicked. She urged Joseph to commit a most grievous crime. He, however, would not consent, and said: "How can I commit so great a sin against my God!"

3. On a certain day the woman took hold of the skirt of his cloak, and tried to keep him. But Joseph left the cloak in her hand, and fled. Thereupon the woman grew very angry. She showed the mantle to her husband, and said: "Joseph came to me, and tried to do me harm. But when I called aloud, he left his garment in my hand and fled."

4. Putiphar believed his wife. He became very angry, and cast Joseph into prison.

QUESTIONS

1. To whom was Joseph sold in Egypt? 2. What did the wife of Putiphar urge Joseph to commit? 3. What did she do on a certain day? What did she say to her husband? 4. Why was Joseph cast into prison?

15. Joseph in Prison

EVEN in prison, God was with Joseph, and caused him to find favor in the sight of the keeper of the jail, who gave Joseph charge of all the other captives. Then it came to pass, that the chief butler and the chief baker of King Pharao were cast into the dungeon.

2. One morning Joseph perceived that these two men were very sad. He asked them: "Why are you so sad?" They answered: "We have dreamed a dream last night, and we have nobody to explain it to us." Joseph said to them: "Does not the interpretation come from God? Tell me what ye have dreamed."

3. The chief butler first told his dream. Joseph answered: "After three days the king will restore thee to thy former place. Remember me then, and ask the king to take me out of this prison, for I am innocent."

4. Then the chief baker related his dream. Joseph said to him: "After three days the king will take thy head from thee, and hang thee on a cross."

5. The third day came. It was the birthday of Pharao. Then the king remembered his chief butler and his chief baker. The former was restored to his place, the latter he caused to be hanged on a gibbet. The chief butler rejoiced in his good fortune; but he thought no more of Joseph.

QUESTIONS

1. How did Joseph find favor with the keeper of the prison? 2. Why were the chief baker and the chief butler sad? 3. What did Joseph tell the chief butler? 4. What did he say to the chief baker? What happened on the third day?

16. The Exaltation of Joseph

AFTER two years Pharao had a dream. He thought he stood by the river Nile. And up came out of the water seven kine, very beautiful and fat, and they fed in marshy places. After them came also seven other kine, that were ill-favored and lean, and they devoured the fat ones. Then the king awoke. He slept again, and dreamed another dream. Seven ears of corn grew up, on one stalk, and the ears were full and fair. After these sprang up seven other ears, thin and blighted, which devoured all the beauty of the former.

2. Thereupon Pharao awoke again. When morning was come, he sent for all the wise men of Egypt, and related to them his dreams. But no one was able to interpret them.

3. Then the chief butler remembered Joseph, and said: "There is in prison a youth, who on one occasion interpreted dreams for me and for the chief baker, and all came to pass in due time." The king sent for Joseph and related to him his two dreams.

4. Joseph said: "The seven beautiful kine, and the seven full ears are seven years of plenty. But the seven lean cows and the seven blighted ears are seven years of famine. Then there will be a great scarcity throughout the country. Therefore, let the king choose a wise man who shall store up in barns the abundance of the seven years of plenty, so that it be ready against the seven years of famine.

5. This counsel was pleasing to the king, and he said to Joseph: "Can I find such another man that is full of the Spirit of God? Thou shalt be over my

JOSEPH IN THE CHARIOT

house, and at the commandment of thy mouth all the people shall obey."

6. Thereupon Pharao took the ring from his own hand, and placed it on Joseph's hand. He also put on him a robe of silk, and placed a chain of gold around his neck. Then he caused Joseph to be seated in a triumphal chariot, and a herald cried out: "Bend your knees to Joseph; for he is the governor of the whole land of Egypt."

QUESTIONS

1. What did Pharao dream about seven kine and seven ears? 2. What did Pharao do in the morning? 3. Whom did the chief butler remember? 4. How did Joseph explain the dreams? 5. What did Pharao then say to Joseph? 6. What did he do to Joseph?

17. The Sons of Jacob Go to Egypt

THE seven years of plenty came, as Joseph had foretold. Joseph gathered all the surplus of the grain, and stored it up in the granaries. But in due time the seven years of scarcity set in, and there was a great famine in all the countries. Then Joseph opened the barns, and provided the whole country with bread.

2. At last the famine prevailed also in the land of Chanaan. Jacob, therefore, said to his sons: "Go ye down into Egypt, and buy what is necessary, that we may not die of hunger." So the ten sons of Jacob went down. But the youngest, called Benjamin, was kept at home by Jacob, lest, perhaps, some evil might befall him on the way.

3. The ten brothers arrived safely in Egypt, and seeing Joseph, they bowed down before him. They knew not that he was their brother. But he recognized them, and remembered his dream. To try them, he spoke harshly to them, and said: "Ye are spies; you are come to explore the country."

4. They answered: "No; it is not so, my lord. We are peaceable men, and have no bad intentions. We are, altogether, twelve brothers. The youngest, however, is with our father at home, and the other . . . is not living."

5. But Joseph replied: "It is as I said: ye are spies." So he cast them into prison for three days.

6. On the third day he brought them out of prison and said: "I will see, whether you speak the truth. Go ye home with your corn, and bring your youngest brother to me. But one of you shall remain in prison until then."

7. Thereupon they said to one another: "We deserve to suffer these things, because we sinned against our brother Joseph. We saw the anguish of his soul, when he besought us, and we would not hear; therefore is this affliction come upon us.

8. The brothers thought that Joseph did not understand them; but he understood all that they said. He turned aside and wept, for his heart was moved to pity. Then he ordered Simeon to be bound before their eyes. He commanded his servants to fill their sacks with corn, and to put each man's money secretly in his bag. This being done, they loaded their asses and returned home.

9. They related to their father all that had happened. But when they opened their sacks, behold! every man found his money tied in the mouth of his sack. All were astonished. But their father Jacob said: "Ye have made me childless. Joseph is not living, Simeon is kept in bonds, and Benjamin ye will take away. My son shall not go down with you; for if any evil befall him, you will bring my gray hairs in sorrow to the grave."

QUESTIONS

1. What did Joseph do during the years of plenty? 2. Why did Jacob send his sons to Egypt? Whom did he keep at home? 3. How did Joseph act towards his brothers? 4. What did they say that they were? 5. How long were they in prison? 6. What did he say to them on the third day? 7. What did the brothers say to one another? 8. What did Joseph say to his servants? 9. What did Jacob exclaim when his sons related all that had happened?

18. Benjamin's Journey to Egypt

IN the meantime the corn which the sons of Jacob had brought from Egypt was consumed, and the famine still continued. Therefore Jacob said to his sons: "Go again to Egypt and bring us a little food." Juda answered: "The man told us expressly, that we should not appear before him again without our youngest brother. Let the boy go with us, lest we perish. I take the risk of the boy upon me."

2. At last the father said to them: "If it must needs be so, do as ye like. Take presents with you for that man, and as much money again as the first time; and besides, the money which ye have found in your sacks. May the almighty God make the man favorable to you, and send back with you Simeon, whom he keeps, and this my dear Benjamin. In the meantime I shall be desolate without children."

3. So they went down to Egypt and stood before the governor. When Joseph saw them and Benjamin in their midst, he said to his steward: "Conduct these men to my house; they shall feast with me." The steward obeyed and brought Simeon out to them.

4. Joseph soon came into the dining-room. His brothers bowed down before him, and offered their gifts. Joseph greeted them kindly, and asked: "Is your aged father yet living? Is he in good health?"

5. They answered: "Our father is yet living and in good health."

Then seeing Benjamin, Joseph asked: "Is this your youngest brother? God bless thee, my son. And he went out in haste weeping; for his heart was deeply moved.

6. He then dried his tears and washed his face, and came in again to his brothers, and said to the servant: "Set bread on the table." But the brothers were seated in the order of age; the first-born first, and the youngest last. They all received gifts; but Benjamin five times more than the others. They wondered very much.

QUESTIONS

1. What did Jacob say to his sons when the corn was consumed? What did Juda answer? 2. What did Jacob then say to them? 3. What did Joseph say when he saw Benjamin in their midst? 4. What did Joseph ask when he came in to his brothers? 5. What did they answer? 6. What did Joseph say to his servants? How were the brothers seated at table? What did they receive?

19. The Silver Cup of Joseph—He Makes Himself Known to His Brothers

JOSEPH showed this preference for Benjamin in order to see, if his brothers had overcome their former feeling of envy. Therefore, the feast being over, he said to his steward: "Fill their sacks with corn, and put each one's money in the top of his sack; and, moreover, place my silver cup in the mouth of the sack of the youngest." This was done, and the brothers set out on their journey. As soon as they had left the city, Joseph said to the steward: "Pursue the men, and say: Why have ye stolen the cup of my master? Ye have done a very evil thing."

2. The steward overtook the brothers, and exclaimed: "Why have you returned evil for good? Why have you stolen the cup?" They were struck

with terror, and they answered: "With whomsoever the cup shall be found, let him die, and we will be the slaves of my lord." The steward searched all the bags, and at last he found the cup in the sack of Benjamin. Then the brothers rent their garments, and returned to the city.

3. When they stood in the presence of Joseph, they fell down before him and said: "Behold, we are all bondmen to my lord!"

4. Joseph replied: "God forbid; but he that stole the cup, he shall be my bondman. You others may return free to your father."

5. Then Juda coming nearer to Joseph, spoke: "I took the boy into my keeping. If we were to return home without him, our father would die of grief. Therefore, I will stay instead of the boy, and I will

JOSEPH EMBRACING BENJAMIN

be thy slave; but let Benjamin go home to his father."

6. Then Joseph could no longer restrain himself. He wept aloud and said: "I am Joseph; is my father yet living?" His brothers could not utter a word, being struck with great fear. Joseph said kindly to them: "Come nearer to me! I am Joseph, your brother, whom ye sold into Egypt. Fear nothing; God sent me before you into Egypt, for your preservation. Make haste and go to my father, and bring him hither. I will feed him during the five years of scarcity that yet remain."

7. Then he fell upon the neck of Benjamin and wept. He kissed his brothers and wept over each of them. After this they were emboldened to speak to him.

8. Joseph gave them carriages and a great many presents. On their departure he warned them not to be angry on the way.

QUESTIONS

1. Why did Joseph show preference to Benjamin? What about the silver cup? 2. What did the steward exclaim? What did they answer? 3. What did they say when they stood before Joseph? 4. What did Joseph reply? 5. What did Juda then say? 6. What did Joseph then do and say?

20. Jacob's Journey to Egypt

WHEN the brothers of Joseph came back to their father, they cried out: "Joseph, thy son, is living, and he is ruler in all the land of Egypt." But Jacob would not believe them. Then they explained to him all that had happened, and they showed him the royal carriages and the presents. Thereupon he exclaimed: "It is enough for me, that Joseph, my son, liveth; I will go and see him before I die." He, therefore, set out for Egypt, taking with him all that he possessed.

2. Juda went on in advance, to tell Joseph that his father was approaching. Joseph made ready his royal chariot and set out to meet his father. As soon as he saw him coming, he descended from his chariot, fell upon his father's neck and wept aloud with joy. Jacob said to Joseph: "Now I shall die with joy, because I have seen thy face and leave thee alive."

3. Joseph gave his father and his brothers possessions in the land of Gessen. This country was very beautiful and abounded in meadows. He also enriched them and allowed food to every one.

4. When Jacob was dead, Joseph wept and mourned for him a long time. Joseph lived one hundred and ten years and saw his children's children to the third generation.

Then he died a happy death, and they embalmed his body, and laid it in a coffin.

QUESTIONS

1. What did the brothers of Joseph say to their father? Did he believe them? 2. Who went in advance? Who made ready his chariot? 3. What did Joseph give to his father, and to his brothers? 4. How long did Joseph live?

21. The Birth of Moses

THE descendants of Jacob became very numerous in Egypt. They were called Israelites because God had given to Jacob the name of Israel. They were also known by the name of Hebrews.

2. Now there arose a new king of Egypt, who knew not Joseph. He oppressed the Israelites with

FINDING OF MOSES IN THE BULRUSHES

burdens and hard labor. At last Pharao said to the Egyptians: "Cast into the river all the male children that are born of Hebrew parents!"

3. Then it came to pass that a Hebrew mother bore a son; and seeing that he was very beautiful, she hid him for three months. But not being able to keep him any longer, she laid the babe in a basket of reeds, and placed it in the sedges of the river. The boy's sister stood a little way off, to see what would happen.

4. But behold! the daughter of Pharao came down to the river. When she saw the basket among the bulrushes, she sent one of her maids to fetch it. On opening the basket she saw a lovely child that was crying piteously. She had compassion on the infant, and said: "Alas! This is one of the Hebrew babes."

5. The child's sister then came up to her and asked: "May I call a Hebrew mother to nurse the babe?"

6. The princess answered: "Yes, go!"

Full of joy, the girl went and called her mother. When the mother of the babe had come, Pharao's daughter said to her: "Take this child and nurse him for me, and I will give thee thy wages."

7. So she took the child and nursed him. And when he had grown up, she brought him to the king's daughter, who adopted him as her son, and said: "His name shall be Moses, for I have rescued him from the waters."

QUESTIONS

1. By what two names were the descendants of Jacob called? 2. What did the new king do to the Israelites? 3. Who gave birth to a man-child? Where did she place the basket? 4. Who came to the river and saw the basket? 5. What did the sister of the child say? 6. What did the princess say to the mother of the child? 7. Who adopted the child when he had grown up? How did she call him?

22. The Flight of Moses—The Burning Bush

MOSES was reared at the court of Pharao, and instructed in all the learning of Egypt. But when he was grown up, and saw the misery of the Israelites, he resolved to help them. So he left the palace of the king, and openly declared himself as the friend of his countrymen. Pharao therefore sought to kill him; but Moses fled into the land of Madian. In this country he came to a priest, called Jethro. He lived with Jethro for forty years, and fed his flocks.

MOSES AT THE BURNING BUSH

2. One day he drove his sheep to the inner parts of the desert. There the Lord appeared to him in a flame of fire, which was in the midst of a bush. Moses saw that the bush was on fire, and yet was not burnt. He wondered at it, and went nearer to see why the bush was not burnt. But the Lord called to him: "Come not nigh hither. Put off the shoes from thy feet; for the ground upon which thou standest is holy. I am the God of thy fathers, the God of Abraham, Issac and Jacob." Moses hid his face, and durst not look at God.

3. Thereupon God said to him: "I have seen the affliction of My people in Egypt, and have heard their crying. I will deliver them out of the hands of the Egyptians, and bring them into the land of Chanaan. I will send thee to Pharao, and thou shalt

lead My people out of Egypt. I will be with thee.

4. Moses answered: "The Israelites will not believe me. They will say: The Lord has not appeared to thee." Then God said to Moses: "Take thy rod and cast it down upon the ground." Moses did so; and the rod was turned into a serpent, so that Moses fled from it in terror. And the Lord said: "Put out thy hand, and take it by the tail." Moses did so; and the serpent became again a rod. Then the Lord spoke again: "Show this sign to the Israelites, and they will believe thee."

5. So Moses returned to Egypt; and Aaron his brother, sent by God, came to meet him. They went together to assemble the people of Israel. Aaron related to them all the words of the Lord; while Moses wrought the sign of the rod and other miracles. Then the people believed, and falling down they adored God.

QUESTIONS

1. Why did Moses leave the palace of the king? Who sought to kill him? Who was Jethro? 2. Whither did Moses drive his sheep one day? What did he see? What did he hear? 3. What did God purpose to do by the hand of Moses? 4. Was Moses willing to go to the Israelites? Why? What happened to his rod? 5. Whom did Moses meet on his return to Egypt? Did the people believe?

23. The Ten Plagues of Egypt

MOSES and Aaron went to Pharao and said: "Thus saith the Lord, the God of Israel: Let My people go out of this country." Pharao proudly answered: "Who is the Lord, that I should hear His voice? I know not the Lord, neither will I let the Israelites go." Aaron, thereupon, cast his rod upon the ground and the rod was turned into a serpent. But Pharao's heart remained hardened.

2. And God sent ten plagues on Pharao and on all Egypt, one more dreadful than the other.

3. First, the water of the river was turned into blood.

4. A few days later frogs came; and after them, gnats; and after the gnats, flies; in so great a number, that the whole country and all the houses swarmed with them.

5. Then a sickness destroyed all the animals belonging to the Egyptians.

6. Next boils and swelling blains came out upon men and beasts.

7. After this a terrible hail-storm struck down herbs and trees, and all that was green in the fields.

8. Then clouds of locusts came upon the land, and devoured all that the hail had left.

9. At last it became so dark for three days that the Egyptians could not see one another nor move about. But where the Israelites lived, there was light.

10. Pharao, however, hardened his heart, and he would not let the people go. Then Moses threatened Pharao with the tenth plague, and said: "In one night all the first-born of the Egyptians shall die."

QUESTIONS

1. What did Pharao say to Moses and Aaron? What did Aaron do? 2. What did God send on Pharao? 3. What was the first plague? 4. What were the second, third and fourth plagues? 5. What happened in the fifth plague? 6. What was the sixth plague? 7, 8, 9. What were the seventh, eighth and ninth plagues? 10. How did Moses threaten Pharao with the tenth plague?

24. The Paschal Lamb

MOSES and Aaron gathered together the people, and spoke to them: "Thus saith the Lord: On the fourteenth day of this month, towards evening, every family shall kill a lamb without blemish. You shall not break a bone of the lamb. You shall take its blood, and with it, you shall sprinkle the posts of your doors. But the flesh of the lamb must be eaten the same night, together with unleavened bread. For on that very night My angel shall slay every first-born of the Egyptians. But when he sees the blood of the lamb on your doors, he shall pass by, and there shall be no mourning nor death in your houses."

2. The night of the fourteenth day came, and the Israelites did as they were commanded. At midnight

EATING THE PASCHAL LAMB AND MARKING THE DOOR-POSTS

the angel of the Lord passed through Egypt and slew every first-born from the king's first-born to the first-born of the laborer. There arose a fearful cry from all the land of Egypt, because death was in every house. But the houses of the Israelites were spared; for the doors were sprinkled with the blood of the lamb. Then the king, calling Moses and Aaron in the night, said: "Go ye forth from among my people, and bless me."

3. The Israelites rose up in haste with all that they possessed. Moses said to them: "This day ye shall celebrate as a feast from generation to generation."

The blood of the paschal lamb was a figure of the blood of Christ.

QUESTIONS

1. What did Moses and Aaron tell the people about the fourteenth day of the month? What about the paschal lamb? Why should they sprinkle their doors with its blood? 2. Who passed through Egypt at midnight? What happened then? 3. What did the Israelites do?

25. The Passage of the Red Sea

NOW God Himself conducted the Israelites in their march. He went before them by day in a pillar of cloud, by night in a pillar of flame. Thus they reached the sea-shore.

2. Now, Pharao repented of allowing the Israelites to depart. So he pursued them with chariots, horsemen and his whole army. At night-fall he overtook them near the Red Sea. The Israelites were seized with great fear, and cried to God for help. But Moses said to them: "Fear not, the Lord will fight for you."

DROWNING OF THE EGYPTIANS

3. And behold! the pillar of cloud arose, and came down between the Israelites and the Egyptians. To the Egyptians it made the night darker, so that they could not see the Israelites. To the Israelites, however, it gave light. Then at the command of God, Moses stretched out his rod over the sea, and immediately the waters divided and stood like a wall on either side. A hot wind dried the ground, and the Israelites marched through the midst of the sea.

4. At the dawn of the next day Pharao pursued the Israelites into the midst of the sea.

But then peals of thunder and flashes of lightning burst forth from the pillar of cloud, and the Lord said to Moses: "Stretch thy hand over the sea." Moses did so. And behold! the divided waters came together again from the right and from the left, covering the chariots, the horsemen and the whole army of Pharao.

5. Thus the Lord miraculously saved the Israelites from the hands of the Egyptians. The people feared the Lord, and believed in Him and in Moses, His servant.

QUESTIONS

1. How did God conduct the Israelites? 2. What did Pharao do? 3. How did the pillar of cloud come down? How were the waters divided? 4. How did Pharao and his army perish? 5. In whom did the people believe?

26. The Miracles Wrought in the Desert

AFTER the people of God had crossed the Red Sea, they came into a desert. There they had

MOSES STRIKING THE ROCK

neither bread nor meat. So they became discontented and murmured. But the Lord said to them: "In the evening ye shall have meat, and in the morning bread."

2. And behold! in the evening quails in great number came into the camp sufficient for all the children of Israel to eat. But in the morning the wilderness was covered with a delicious food which looked like hoar-frost. It was manna. It had a sweet taste like flour mixed with honey. With this bread God fed the Israelites for forty years, until they entered the land of Chanaan.

3. Some time after this the Israelites came to another part of the desert. There they found no water, and again they murmured against Moses. The Lord said to Moses: "Take thy rod, go to Mount Horeb, strike the rock, and water will flow from it." Moses did so, and a stream of water burst forth, so that the people and the cattle could quench their thirst at will.

QUESTIONS

1. What was wanting to the people in the desert? 2. What came in the evening into the camp? What fell in the morning? 3. What happened when the people found no water?

27. The Ten Commandments

IN the third month the Israelites came to Mount Sinai. There they pitched their tents. Moses ascended the mountain, and the Lord said to him: "Go down to the people, and command them to purify themselves to-day and to-morrow, to wash their garments, and to be ready on the third day. When the trumpet sounds, they shall all come to the

MOSES RECEIVING THE TABLES OF THE LAW

foot of the mountain." Moses did as the Lord had commanded him.

2. The third morning came, and there was thunder and lightning. A thick cloud covered the whole mountain, and smoke mixed with flames arose from the summit. The trumpet sounded very loud, and the earth rocked and trembled. The people below on the plain feared exceedingly.

3. And Moses led them to the foot of the mount, and God spoke out of the cloud:

I. I am the Lord, thy God. Thou shalt not have strange gods before Me; thou shalt not make to thyself a graven thing, to adore it!

II. Thou shalt not take the name of the Lord, thy God, in vain!

III. Remember that thou keep holy the Sabbath-day!
IV. Honor thy father and thy mother, that thou mayest be long-lived upon the land!
V. Thou shalt not kill!
VI. Thou shalt not commit adultery!
VII. Thou shalt not steal!
VIII. Thou shalt not bear false witness against thy neighbor!
IX. Thou shalt not covet thy neighbor's wife!
X. Thou shalt not covet thy neighbor's goods!

Then the people, full of awe, cried out: "We will do all that the Lord has spoken."

4. Afterwards Moses went again on the mount, and stayed there for forty days and forty nights. He ate no bread, and drank no water. There the Lord gave him two stone tables, on which the hand of God had written the Ten Commandments.

QUESTIONS

1. What did God say to Moses when the people came to Mount Sinai? 2. What happened on the third morning? 3. Say the Ten Commandments. 4. How long did Moses stay on the Mountain?

28. The Israelites in the Promised Land—The Heathen Nations

AFTER forty years the Israelites entered the land of Chanaan. Here they dwelt, and built towns and villages. Their capital was Jerusalem. Solomon, one of their kings, erected a magnificent temple there. In it was the sanctuary, and the Holy of the

Holies. In the sanctuary, the priests offered their sacrifices. In the Holy of the Holies, the High-Priest, alone, entered once a year.

2. Afterwards the Israelites were also called Jews. They were the only people that believed in the one true God. All other nations were heathens or idolaters. They worshipped false gods, and led a very bad life. They were very unhappy.

3. The Jews believed in God, and waited for the coming of the Savior. But only a small portion of them kept the Commandments. The others had no fear of God; they committed great sins and many crimes. In this manner time went on. At last the world was filled with wickedness, sin, and misery.

4. Men were helpless and knew of no remedy. Then God had pity on them, and sent His only begotten Son from heaven to redeem mankind.

QUESTIONS

1. What did the Israelites build in the promised land? 2. What was the faith of the Jews? What that of the heathen nations? 2. Did all the Jews keep ·the Commandments? 4. Whom did God send when men were helpless?

SECOND PART

HISTORY OF THE NEW TESTAMENT

---

1. The Birth of John the Baptist is Announced

DURING the reign of King Herod, there lived in the mountains of Judea a priest called Zachary. The name of his wife was Elizabeth. They were both just, and faithfully kept all commandments of the Lord. They had no children, and were advanced in years.

ZACHARY AND THE ANGEL

2. One day Zachary had to perform the priestly office. He went into the temple and stood before the altar with the censer. The people were praying outside the sanctuary. Suddenly Zachary saw an angel standing at the side of the altar. Zachary was afraid. But the angel said to him: "Fear not, Zachary! Thy prayer is heard; thy wife Elizabeth shall bear thee a son, and thou shalt call his name John. Thou shalt have joy and gladness; for he shall be great before the Lord. He will drink no wine, nor strong drink. He shall be filled with the Holy Ghost before his birth, and he shall convert many of the children of Israel to the Lord their God. And he will go before Him to prepare for the Lord a perfect people." The angel then disappeared, and Zachary returned home.

QUESTIONS

1. What is said of Zachary and Elizabeth? 2. What did Zachary do in the temple? Who appeared to him? What did the angel say?

2. The Angel Gabriel Announces the Birth of Christ

SIX months after this the Angel Gabriel was sent to Nazareth to a virgin, whose name was Mary, and who was espoused to a man, called Joseph. The angel came to Mary, and said: "Hail Mary! full of grace, the Lord is with thee; blessed art thou among women."

2 When Mary heard these words she was troubled. But the angel said to her: "Fear not, Mary! for thou hast found grace with God; thou shalt have a son, and thou shalt call His name Jesus. He shall

THE ANNUNCIATION

be great and be called the Son of the Most High." Mary said to the angel: "How is this to happen?"

3. The angel replied: "The Holy Ghost shall come upon thee, and the power of the Most High shall overshadow thee. And behold! thy cousin Elizabeth, she also hath conceived a son in her old age; for with God nothing is impossible."

4. Mary answered: "Behold the handmaid of the Lord; be it done to me according to thy word." Then the angel departed from her.

5. Afterwards the angel appeared to Joseph, and said to him: "Joseph, fear not to take unto thee Mary, thy wife. The Holy Ghost has come upon her, and she shall bear a son. Thou shalt call His name Jesus, for He shall save His people from their sins."

QUESTIONS

1. To what virgin was the Angel Gabriel sent? 2. What did the angel say when Mary was troubled? 3. What did the angel say about the Holy Ghost, and about Elizabeth? 4. What did Mary answer? 5. What did the angel say to Joseph?

3. Mary Visits Her Cousin Elizabeth

MARY arose in those days, and went with haste to the hill country to visit her cousin Elizabeth. No sooner did Mary enter into the house than Elizabeth, filled with the Holy Ghost, cried out with a loud voice: "Blessed art thou among women, and blessed is the fruit of thy womb. And whence is this

THE VISITATION OF ST. ELIZABETH

to me, that the mother of my Lord should come to me!"

2. Whereupon Mary exclaimed: "My soul doth magnify the Lord, and my spirit rejoiceth in God my Savior. Because He has looked down on the lowliness of His handmaid: for behold! henceforth all generations shall call me blessed." Mary stayed about three months with Elizabeth; then she returned home.

3. And Elizabeth bore a son as the angel had foretold. Zachary and Elizabeth rejoiced and called the child's name John, as the Angel Gabriel had commanded. But the boy grew, and was strengthened in spirit. He went into the desert and abode there until he was called to manifest himself to Israel.

QUESTIONS

1. Where did Mary go in those days? 2. What did Mary exclaim? 3. Why did Zachary and Elizabeth rejoice? Where did John abide?

4. The Birth of Jesus Christ

IN those days a decree went forth from the Roman emperor Augustus, commanding that all the subjects of his empire should be enrolled. Each tribe to be enrolled in the city to which they belonged.

2. Joseph and Mary went to Bethlehem, the city of David, because they belonged to the tribe of David. But there was no room for them in the inn. Therefore they left the town, and took shelter in a stable. There, in that poor stable, Jesus Christ, the Son of God, was born. Mary wrapped the child in swaddling-clothes, and laid Him in a manger.

QUESTIONS

1. What decree went forth? 2. Why did Joseph and Mary go to Bethlehem? Why did they leave the town? Where was the Savior born?

5. An Angel Announces to the Shepherds the Birth of Christ

IN THE same night some shepherds kept watch over their flocks. Suddenly an angel of the Lord appeared to them, and said: "Fear not. I bring you good tidings of great joy. This night is born to you, in the city of David, a Savior, who is Christ the Lord. This shall be a sign to you: You shall find a babe wrapped in swaddling-clothes and lying in a manger."

THE ADORATION OF THE SHEPHERDS

2. And immediately there was with the angel a multitude of the heavenly hosts. They praised the Lord and sang: "Glory be to God on high, and on earth peace to men of good will." Then the angels returned into heaven, and the shepherds said to one another: "Let us go over to Bethlehem, and see what the Lord has told us."

3. They went in haste, and found Mary and Joseph and the babe lying in a manger. Then they adored the child, and returned home praising and glorifying God. Eight days after the child was circumcised, and His name was called Jesus, as the angel had commanded.

QUESTIONS

1. Who were keeping watch that same night? 2. Who were suddenly with the angel? What did the shepherds say after the angels had returned into heaven? 3. Whom did they find? What happened eight days after?

6. The Adoration of the Three Wise Men from the East

WHEN Jesus was born at Bethlehem, three wise men, or kings, came from the East to Jerusalem. They asked: "Where is the new-born King of the Jews? We have seen His star in the East, and we are come to adore Him." Now Herod, the king, hearing this, was troubled. He assembled all the chief scribes and inquired of them where Christ was to be born. They said: "In Bethlehem, of Juda."

2. Then Herod sent the three wise men to Bethlehem, and said to them: "Go and search diligently after the child, and when ye have found Him, bring me word again, that I also may come and adore Him."

THE ADORATION OF THE MAGI

3. The Magi immediately set out for Bethlehem. And, behold! the star went before them till it stood over the place where the child was. When they saw the star they were pleased. They entered in, and found Jesus and Mary, His mother. They fell down and adored the child. They also offered Him gifts: gold, frankincense and myrrh.

4. In the night God warned the Magi not to return to Herod. Therefore they went back by another way to their country.

QUESTIONS

1. Who came from the East to Jerusalem? 2. What did Herod say then to the three wise men? 3. What did the Magi do when they entered in? 4. How did God warn the Magi?

7. Jesus is Presented in the Temple

WHEN Jesus was forty days old, Mary and Joseph brought Him to Jerusalem to present Him to the Lord. They carried with them a pair of young turtle-doves, an offering which the very poorest were obliged to make.

2. There lived in Jerusalem at that time a very devout man, named Simeon. He was longing for the coming of the Messias. Led by the Holy Spirit, Simeon came into the temple at the time when Mary and Joseph brought in the child Jesus. He took Him in his arms, blessed God and said: "Now I can die in peace, for my eyes have seen the Savior."

3. There lived also in Jerusalem a widow, eighty-four years of age. Her name was Anna. She served

THE PRESENTATION

God, and prayed and fasted day and night. She also came in at the same hour, praised the Lord and spoke of Jesus to all that were expecting the Savior.

QUESTIONS

1. What happened when Jesus was forty days old? 2. Who was Simeon? What did he do? 3. What widow was also living in Jerusalem? What did she do?

8. The Flight Into Egypt

SOME time after the angel of the Lord appeared to Joseph, and said: "Arise, take the child and His mother, and flee into Egypt. Stay there until I shall tell thee. Herod will seek the child to kill Him." Joseph arose, took the child and His mother, and went into Egypt.

THE HOLY FAMILY IN NAZARETH

2. Herod was still waiting for the return of the wise men. At last, when they did not come, he grew very angry. He ordered that all the male children in Bethlehem and its neighborhood from two years and less should be killed. So it was done. Then there arose a great lamentation, and the mothers would not be comforted.

3. Some years later, Herod died a terrible death. Then the angel of the Lord appeared to Joseph in Egypt, and said to him: "Arise, take the child and His mother, and go into the land of Israel." Joseph arose, took the child and His mother and went to the land of Israel. He retired to Galilee, and lived in Nazareth.

QUESTIONS

1. Who appeared to Joseph soon after? 2. For what was Herod still waiting? What order did he give? 3. Who appeared to Joseph when Herod was dead?

9. The Child Jesus Remains Three Days in the Temple

WHEN Jesus was twelve years old, He went with His parents to Jerusalem. The holy days of Easter being over, Mary and Joseph returned home. But Jesus remained in Jerusalem, and His parents knew it not. They made a day's journey, and sought Jesus among their relatives and neighbors. As they did not find Him, they returned to Jerusalem. They were in great sorrow and affliction.

2. After seeking for three days they found Him in the temple. He was sitting in the midst of the doctors, listening to them and asking them questions. And all, that heard Him, were astonished at His wisdom and His questions.

JESUS AMONGST THE DOCTORS

3. His mother said to Him: "Son, why hast Thou done this to us? Behold, Thy father and I have sought Thee sorrowing." Jesus answered: "Why did ye seek Me? Did ye not know that I must be about the things of My Father?"

4. He arose and returned home with His parents to Nazareth, and was subject to them. He grew in wisdom and grace before God and men. He stayed with His parents at Nazareth till the beginning of His public life.

QUESTIONS

1. What happened when Jesus was twelve years old? 2. Where did Mary and Joseph find Him? 3. What did His mother say to Him? 4. Whither did He go with them?

10. John the Baptist, Precursor of Jesus, Preaches and Baptizes

THE time was now drawing near when Jesus should manifest Himself to the world. Then John began to preach and baptize in the country about the river Jordan. He said: "Do penance, for the kingdom of God is at hand."

2. John was clothed in a garment of camel's hair, and wore a leather girdle round his loins. His food was wild honey and locusts. The inhabitants of Jerusalem, and of the whole land of Judea, came to the river to John. They were baptized, and confessed their sins.

3. Now, many people thought that he was the promised Redeemer. John said, therefore: "I am not Christ, but after me there will come He, who is more powerful than I. I baptize in water, but He will baptize you in the Holy Spirit."

QUESTIONS

1. When did John begin to preach? 2. How was John clothed? What did the inhabitants of Jerusalem do? 3. What did many people think of John?

11. Jesus is Baptized by John

AT that time Jesus came from Nazareth to the river Jordan, in order to be baptized by John. At first John would not baptize Him, but said: "I ought to be baptized by Thee, and comest Thou to me?" But Jesus said to him: "Suffer it now; God so willeth it." Then John did as he was commanded.

2. When Jesus was baptized, He came out of the water and prayed. And, behold! the heavens were

THE BAPTISM OF CHRIST

opened, and the Holy Ghost came down upon Him in the shape of a dove. Moreover, a voice from heaven was heard, saying: "This is My beloved Son, in Whom I am well pleased."

QUESTIONS

1. *What did John say when Jesus wished to be baptized?*
2. *What occurred after Christ was baptized?*

12. Jesus Works His First Miracle at a Wedding in Cana

WHEN Jesus was thirty years old, He began to teach publicly and to work miracles. He also gathered disciples around Him. And from the disciples He chose twelve whom He called apostles.

2. Jesus worked His first miracle in Cana, a small town of Galilee. There was a wedding, and Mary was there. Jesus and His disciples were likewise among the guests.

3. When Mary saw that the wine began to fail, she said to Jesus: "They have no wine." Jesus answered: "My hour is not yet come." But Mary said to the waiters: "Whatsoever He shall say to you, do ye."

4. There were in the room six stone pitchers, containing two or three measures apiece. Jesus said to the waiters: "Fill the pitchers with water." And they filled them up to the brim. Then Jesus said to them: "Draw out now, and carry it to the chief steward." And they carried it.

CHANGING WATER INTO WINE

5. The chief steward tasted the water that had been turned into wine. But he did not know where the wine came from. He therefore called the bridegroom and said to him: "Every man at first sets forth the good wine and then that which is worse; but thou has kept the good wine until now."

6. Jesus wrought His first miracle in Cana of Galilee at the request of His blessed mother. His disciples seeing His divine power believed in Him.

QUESTIONS

1. What did Jesus do when He was thirty years of age? 2. Where did He work His first miracle? 3. What did Mary say to Jesus? 4. How many pitchers were standing there? What did Jesus say to the waiters? 5. What did the chief steward say? 6. Why did the disciples believe in Him?

13. Jesus Teaches the People, and Heals the Sick

ON a Sabbath day Jesus was teaching in the synagogue in Capharnaum. From the synagogue He went to the house of Simon Peter and Andrew, his brother. Peter's mother-in-law was suffering from a dangerous fever, and they asked the Lord to cure her. Jesus drew near to her bed, took her by the hand and commanded the fever. Immediately she arose being cured of the sickness and waited on Jesus and His disciples.

2. After sunset, the sick and infirm of the whole city were brought to Jesus. He laid His hand on every one of them and healed them.

3. Jesus wandered about in the whole land of Galilee and preached. He said to the people: "Do pen-

THE SICK BROUGHT TO JESUS

ance and believe." All those that were suffering from sickness or disease were brought to Him, and He cured them all.

QUESTIONS

1. Who was sick in the house of Peter and Andrew? 2. What did Christ do after sunset? 3. What did Jesus preach in Galilee?

14. Jesus Raises from the Dead the Son of the Widow of Naim

IT came to pass one day, that Jesus went into a city called Naim. And there went with Him His disciples, and a great crowd of people. As He came near the gate of the city, behold! a dead man was carried out, the only son of a widow. The poor mother, full of sorrow, walked after the bier, and a great many people of the city accompanied her.

2. Jesus, seeing the bereaved mother, was moved with compassion towards her, and said: "Weep not!" Then He made a sign to the bearers to stop, and coming up, He touched the bier and said: "Young man, I say to thee, arise." And he that had been dead sat up, and began to speak. And Jesus gave him to his mother.

3. All those who witnessed this great miracle were seized with fear. They glorified God, saying: "A great prophet is risen up amongst us, and God has visited His people."

QUESTIONS

1. What did Jesus meet in the gate of the city of Naim? 2. What did Jesus say to the mother? What to the dead man? 3. What did the people say?

15. Jesus Stills the Tempest

JESUS on one occasion went to the lake of Genesareth. And great crowds of people followed Him. Jesus went up into a boat to sit down there; the people remained on the shore. And He taught them from the ship.

2. When the night had set in, Jesus said to His disciples: "Let us pass over to the other side." So they sailed across the lake, Jesus being in the ship. But He, wearied and fatigued, began to sleep.

3. And behold! a great storm arose on the sea, and the small vessel was tossed about and covered with the waves. But Jesus was asleep. And the disciples went to Him, awoke Him and said: "Lord, save us, or we perish."

CHRIST STILLING THE TEMPEST

4. Jesus arose and said to them: "Why are you fearful, am I not with you?" Then, rising up, He commanded the wind to cease, and the sea to be still. And behold! there was a great calm. Then all the men wondered, saying: "Who is this? for even the wind and the sea obey Him."

QUESTIONS

1. Where did Jesus sit down to teach the people? 2. What did He tell His disciples? 3. What happened then? 4. What did Jesus say and do? What did the men say?

16. Jesus Feeds the Five Thousand with Five Loaves

ON another occasion Jesus crossed the lake and retired to a desert place. But even there crowds of people followed Him. Jesus had pity on them, taught them, and healed the sick that were brought to Him.

2. Now evening had set in, and the apostles said to Jesus: "Send away the people that they may go into the villages around, and buy provisions."

3. Jesus asked: "How many loaves have ye?" Andrew answered: "There is a boy here who has five loaves and two fishes. But what is this for so many?" Jesus said: "Bring me the loaves and fishes, and make the people sit down on the grass."

4. And when the people sat down, there were five-thousand men, besides women and children. Jesus then took the five loaves and the two fishes, and looking up to heaven, He blessed them, broke the loaves, and gave them to His apostles to distribute among

CHRIST BLESSING THE LOAVES

the people. The fishes were likewise distributed. Now all the people ate and were satisfied.

5. After the multitude had finished eating, Jesus said to His disciples: "Gather the remaining pieces of bread, lest they be wasted." The disciples gathered the remnants which were left of the five loaves and of the two fishes. It was enough to fill twelve baskets. The people, seeing this miracle, exclaimed: "Verily, this is the prophet that is to come into the world."

QUESTIONS

1. Who followed Jesus to the desert place? 2. What did the apostles say in the evening? 3. What did Jesus ask? 4. How many men were there? What did Jesus do with the loaves and the fishes? 5. Who gathered the remnants? What did the people exclaim?

17. Jesus Teaches His Disciples to Pray

ONE day when Jesus had been praying one of His disciples came to Him, saying: "Lord, teach us to pray?"

2. And Jesus said to them: "When you pray, say: Our Father who art in heaven, hallowed be Thy name; Thy kingdom come; Thy will be done on earth, as it is in heaven. Give us this day our daily bread. And forgive us our trespasses, as we forgive those who trespass against us. And lead us not into temptation; but deliver us from evil."

3. He then said to His disciples: "Ask, and it shall be given to you; seek and you shall find, knock, and it shall be opened to you. For every one who asks, receives; and who seeks, finds; and to him who knocks, it shall be opened."

QUESTIONS

1. What did one of the disciples one day say to Jesus? 2. Say the Our Father! 3. What else did Jesus say about prayer?

18. Jesus Tells the Parable of Dives and Lazarus

THERE were also misers among the people that listened to Jesus. He said to them: "There was a certain rich man named Dives. He was clothed in purple and fine linen, and feasted sumptuously every day. And there was a certain poor man, called Lazarus. He lay at the gate of the rich man and was covered with sores. He would have liked to satisfy his hunger with the crumbs that fell from the table of the rich man; but none gave them to him. But the

DIVES AND LAZARUS

dogs came and licked his sores."

2. "Now it came to pass, that the beggar died, and he was carried by the angels into the bosom of Abraham. The rich man also died, and he was buried in hell. And lifting up his eyes, when he was in torments, he saw Abraham afar off, and Lazarus in his bosom."

3. "Then he cried: 'Father Abraham, have pity on me, and send Lazarus, that he may dip the tip of his finger in water, to cool my tongue, for I am tormented in this flame.'"

4. "Abraham said to him: 'Remember that thou didst receive good things in thy lifetime, and Lazarus, on the contrary, evil things. But now he is comforted, and thou art tormented. And besides all this, between us and you there is fixed a great chaos, so that no one can pass from hence to you.'"

QUESTIONS

1. Tell the parable of Dives and Lazarus. 2. What happened to Lazarus after death, and what to Dives? 3. What did Dives ask of Abraham? 4. What did Abraham answer?

19. Jesus Blesses Little Children

ON one occasion some pious mothers brought their children to Jesus, that He might place His hands upon them and bless them. But the apostles did not like this. They would not let the children come near to the Savior. They began to rebuke the mothers, and sent them away with their children.

2. But Jesus said to His disciples: "Suffer little children to come to Me, and forbid them not, for of such is the kingdom of heaven."

CHRIST BLESSING CHILDREN

3. Then Jesus called the children, took them in His arms, laid His hand upon them and blessed them.

QUESTIONS

1. What did some pious mothers do on one occasion? 2. What did Jesus say to His disciples? 3. What did Jesus do?

20. Jesus Raises Lazarus from the Dead

THERE lived in Bethania, near Jerusalem, two sisters, named Mary and Martha. They had an only brother, whose name was Lazarus. He suddenly fell sick, and his sisters sent to Jesus, saying: "Lord, he whom Thou lovest is sick." Jesus remained for two more days where He was. On the third day He said to His disciples: "Lazarus is dead. I will go, and raise him from the dead."

THE RAISING OF LAZARUS

2. When Jesus arrived, Lazarus had been already four days buried. Martha went out to meet Jesus, and said: "Lord, if Thou hadst been here, my brother would not have died." Jesus said to her: "Thy brother will rise again." Martha answered: "I know that he will rise again in the resurrection at the last day."

3. Jesus said to her: "I am the resurrection and the life. He that believeth in Me, although he be dead, shall live. Believest thou this?" She replied: "Lord, I believe that Thou art the Christ, the Son of the Living God, that has come into this world."

4. Then Martha went to call her sister, Mary Magdalen, saying: "The Master is come, and calls for thee." Mary rose up quickly, and went to Jesus. She fell at His feet, and said: "Lord, if Thou hadst been

here, my brother would not have died." Mary began to weep, and all the friends, who had come with her, were moved to pity. And Jesus asked: "Where have ye laid him?" They said: "Come and see." And Jesus wept. The Jews seeing this, exclaimed: "Behold how He loved him."

5. The grave was in a vault, and was covered with a stone. Jesus having come to the sepulcher, said: "Take away the stone." Martha replied: "Lord, he is already putrid, for he is now dead four days." But Jesus said to her: "Did I not tell thee that if thou wilt believe, thou shalt see the glory of God?"

6. Thereupon they removed the stone. Then Jesus lifting up His eyes to heaven, prayed, and crying out with a loud voice He said: "Lazarus, come forth." Immediately he that had been dead came forth from the grave. He had his hands and feet bound with winding bands. Therefore Jesus said to them: "Loose the bands, and let him go."

7. Many of the Jews who were present, believed in Jesus. Others went to the Pharisees, and told them what Jesus had done. Then the Pharisees and scribes exclaimed: "What shall we do? for this man works many miracles." From that day they resolved to put Him to death. But Jesus, knowing their thoughts, retired to a desert place.

QUESTIONS

1. Who lived in Bethania, and who fell ill? 2. What did Martha say to Jesus? 3. What did Jesus answer? 4. Whom did Martha call? What did Mary do and say? 5. What happened at the grave? 6. How was Lazarus raised from the dead? 7. Did some of the Jews believe? Did others go to the Pharisees?

21. Jesus Gives the Commandment of Love

WHEN the Easter of the Jews was near, Jesus went to Jerusalem. As He was preaching in the temple one of the Pharisees asked him: "Which is the greatest commandment in the law?"

2. Jesus said: "Thou shalt love the Lord thy God with thy whole heart, and with thy whole soul, with thy whole mind and with thy whole strength: This is the greatest and first commandment. The other is equal to this: Thou shalt love thy neighbor as thyself."

QUESTIONS

1. About what Commandment was Jesus asked? 2. What did Jesus say?

22. Jesus Describes the Last Judgment

JESUS also foretold His disciples what would happen at the end of the world. He said: "The Son of man shall come in His majesty, and all the angels with Him. Then He shall sit upon the throne of His glory. All the nations of the world will be gathered together before Him, and He will separate the good from the bad, as the shepherd separates the sheep from the goats. He will set the sheep on His right hand, but the goats on His left."

2. "Then will the King say to those on His right hand: 'Come, ye blessed of My Father, possess the kingdom prepared for you, from the foundation of the world.'"

3. "Then He will say to those on the left hand: 'Depart from Me, ye cursed, into everlasting fire, which was prepared for the Devil and his angels.'

And these shall go into everlasting torments, but the just into everlasting life."

QUESTIONS

1. What did Jesus foretell about the end of the world? 2. What will the King say to the just? 3. What will He say to those on His left hand?

23. Jesus Institutes the Most Holy Sacrament of the Altar

AT the last supper before his death, Jesus instituted the Most Holy Sacrament of the Altar. On that night Jesus took the bread in His venerable and holy hands, and raising His eyes to heaven. He blessed the bread, and broke it and gave it to His dis-

THE LAST SUPPER

ciples, saying: "Take ye, and eat; this is My body, which is given for you."

2. In like manner, Jesus also took the chalice, gave thanks, blessed it and gave it to His disciples, saying: "Take ye, and drink ye all of this; for this is My blood, which shall be shed for you and for many for the remission of sins. Do this for a commemoration of Me."

QUESTIONS

1. What did Jesus institute the night before His death?
2. What did Jesus say when He took the chalice?

24. The Agony of Jesus in the Garden

NOW Satan had inspired Judas, one of the twelve apostles, to betray his Lord and Master. Judas went to the scribes, and said to them: "What will you give me, and I will deliver Him unto you?" They promised him thirty pieces of silver. Judas accepted this offer.

2. After Jesus had instituted the Holy Eucharist He went forth with His disciples to Mount Olivet, where there was a garden, called Gethsemane. When Jesus was at the entrance of the garden, He said to His disciples: "Sit you here, while I go yonder and pray." Only Peter, James and John accompanied Him into the garden.

3. Then Jesus began to be sad, and to tremble, and He said: "My soul is sorrowful, even unto death. Stay ye here, and watch, and pray with Me." And He went a little further, fell upon His face, and prayed: "My Father, if it be possible, let this chalice pass from Me. Nevertheless, not as I will, but as Thou wilt."

THE AGONY IN THE GARDEN

4. Thus Jesus prayed three times, and fell into an agony, and His sweat became as drops of blood, trickling down to the ground. He prayed long and fervently. And behold! there appeared an angel, who strengthened Him. Then Jesus arose, and said to His disciples: "Arise, he is at hand who will betray Me."

QUESTIONS

1. To whom did Judas go to betray Jesus? 2. Where did Jesus go with His disciples? 3. How did Jesus pray? 4. How many times did He pray? What of His bloody sweat?

25. Jesus is Seized

WHILE Jesus was yet speaking, Judas came with a great crowd of soldiers and servants. They had lanterns, torches, swords and clubs. Judas had told them: "Whom I shall kiss, that is He; hold Him fast."

2. And the traitor came up to Jesus, and said: "Hail, Rabbi," and he kissed Him. Jesus said to him: "Friend, whereto art thou come? Judas, dost thou betray the Son of man with a kiss?"

3. Then Jesus drew near the crowd, and asked: "Whom seek you?" They replied: "Jesus of Nazareth." Jesus answered: "I am He." And they started back, and fell to the ground, like dead.

4. But Jesus asked again: "Whom seek you?" They answered: "Jesus of Nazareth." Jesus said: "I have told you that I am He. If, therefore, you seek Me, let these go their way." They then laid hands on Him. But Peter, drawing his sword, struck the servant of the high priest, and cut off his right ear. That servant's name was Malchus. Jesus said to Peter: "Put up thy sword into the scabbard." He then touched the ear of Malchus and healed it.

5. They then seized Jesus and bound Him. And His disciples left Him and fled. Only Peter and John followed Him from afar.

QUESTIONS

1. Who came with a great crowd of soldiers? 2. What did Judas say to Jesus? 3. What did Jesus say to the Jews? 4. What did Jesus ask them again? What happened to them? What of Peter? 5. How did the disciples act when Jesus was bound?

26. Jesus is Sentenced to Death by the Council

THE band of soldiers and servants led Jesus to Caiphas, the high priest. He had assembled all the members of the grand council. The high priest and the council tried to find witnesses against Jesus to put Him to death. But they found none.

2. At last Caiphas rose up, and said: "I adjure Thee by the living God, that Thou tell us, whether Thou be the Christ, the Son of the living God." Jesus answered: "Yes, I am He." Then the high priest rent his garments saying: "He has blasphemed. What think you?" They answered: "He is guilty of death."

3. Jesus then was led away and watched until morning. During this time of the night the guards of the tribunal mocked Him. They spat in His face, blindfolded Him, struck Him, and blasphemed Him.

4. But Judas repented of having betrayed Jesus. He brought the thirty pieces of silver back to the scribes, saying: "I have sinned in betraying the innocent Jesus." The scribes answered: "What is that to us: look thou to it." Then casting down the money in the temple Judas went away, out of the city, and hanged himself with a halter.

QUESTIONS

1. Why had the high priest assembled the council? 2. How did Caiphas adjure Jesus? 3. What was done to Jesus during the rest of the night? 4. What about Judas?

27. Jesus is Scourged

AT that time Pontius Pilate was governor in Judea. The Jews led Jesus to him early in the morning to have Him tried. But Pilate knew that Jesus had been delivered by envy of the priests and

THE SCOURGING AT THE PILLAR

Pharisees. He, therefore, wished to save Him from their hands. The priests, however, stirred up the people, and all cried out; "Crucify Him, crucify Him!"

2. Pilate said: "What evil hath He done? I find no cause of death in Him. I will, therefore, scourge Him, and let Him go." And Jesus was led away, stripped of His garments, tied to a pillar and scourged in a most cruel manner.

QUESTIONS

1. Why was Jesus led to Pilate? What did Pilate wish to do? 2. What did Pilate say? What did he order to be done to Jesus?

28. Jesus is Crowned With Thorns

AFTER Jesus had been scourged, the soldiers put an old purple garment about Him. They platted a crown of thorns, put it on His head, and placed a reed in His right hand. Then bowing the knee before Him they mocked Him, saying: "Hail, King of the Jews." Others spat on Him, and took the reed, and struck His head. At last they blindfolded Him and renewed all manner of insult and injury.

QUESTION

What did the soldiers do to Jesus after He had been scourged?

29. Jesus is Shown to the People and Condemned to Death

ONCE more Pilate endeavored to save Jesus. He brought Him out before the people. There the Savior stood with the crown of thorns on His head and wearing the purple garment. And Pilate said: "Behold the man!"

2. But the priests and Pharisees cried out: "Crucify Him, crucify Him!" Pilate answered: "I find no cause in Him." The Jews replied: "We have a law and according to that law He must die: for He said that He was the Son of God."

3. Now for the last time Pilate sought to release Jesus from their hands. But the Jews exclaimed: "If thou let this man go, thou canst be no friend of the emperor."

BEHOLD THE MAN

4. Then Pilate took water, washed his hands saying: "I am innocent of the blood of this just man. Look ye to it." They all cried out: "His blood be upon us and upon our children." Then Pilate delivered Jesus to the Jews to be crucified.

QUESTIONS

1. How was Jesus shown to the people? 2. What did the crowd cry out? What did Pilate say? 3. What did Pilate for the last time seek to do? 4. What did Pilate say when he washed his hands? What did the Jews cry out?-

30. Jesus Carries His Heavy Cross

THE soldiers now seized Jesus. They took off His purple robe and put on Him His own garments. Then they led Him away to crucify Him. Jesus car-

JESUS FALLING UNDER THE CROSS

ried the heavy cross on His shoulders.

2. Thus He went through the streets of Jerusalem towards Mount Calvary, where He was to be crucified. Two robbers were also led out to be crucified with Him.

3. A man, named Simon, happened to pass by, coming from the field. The soldiers seized him, and forced him to help Jesus to carry the cross.

4. A crowd of people followed Jesus. Among them were also some pious women, who bewailed Jesus and shed tears of compassion.

QUESTIONS

1. What did the soldiers do to Jesus? How did Jesus carry His cross? 2. Who were led out with Jesus? 3. What about a man named Simon? 4. What were the pious women doing?

31. Jesus is Crucified

AT noon Jesus reached the top of Mount Calvary. There the soldiers offered Him some wine mingled with gall. Jesus tasted it, but refused to drink. They then nailed Him to the cross.

THE CRUCIFIXION

2. With Him were crucified the two thieves; the one on the right, the other on the left. And the soldiers took His garments, divided them into four parts, one part for each of them. But His coat, being without seam, they would not divide. They, therefore, cast lots for it. Then they sat down to watch Jesus.

QUESTIONS

1. What did the soldiers do when Jesus reached Mount Calvary? 2. Who were crucified with Him? What did the soldiers do?

32. Jesus Speaks His Last Seven Words and Dies

THE priests and the Jews mocked Jesus, saying: "If Thou be the Son of God, come down from the cross! He saved others, Himself He cannot save!" And Jesus spoke: "Father, forgive them, for they know not what they do."

2. One of the thieves who was crucified with Him blasphemed Jesus saying: "If Thou be Christ, save Thyself and us." But the other rebuked him, and exclaimed: "We indeed suffer justly, but He has done no evil." Then he asked Jesus: "Lord, remember me when Thou shalt come into Thy kingdom." Jesus answered: "I say to thee: This day thou shalt be with Me in Paradise."

3. Now there stood near the cross Mary, the mother of Jesus, and John, the disciple whom He especially loved. Jesus said to His mother: "Woman, behold thy son." And to John He said: "Behold thy mother." From that hour John took the mother of Jesus to himself, as if she were his own mother.

4. When noon had come, behold! a great darkness covered all the earth, and lasted for three hours. And Jesus cried out with a loud voice: "My God, My God, why hast Thou forsaken Me?"

5. Soon afterwards Jesus exclaimed: "I thirst." Then a soldier took a sponge, dipped it in vinegar, put it on a reed, and gave Him to drink. After He had taken the vinegar Jesus said: "It is consummated." Then He cried out with a loud voice: "Father, into Thy hands I commend My spirit." Saying this, He bowed His head, and gave up the ghost.

6. And behold! the earth quaked, and the rocks were rent. Many graves were opened, and many bodies of the saints arose. The captain and the sol-

diers, who were watching Jesus, were seized with terror and said: "Indeed, this man was just; He was the Son of God." And the people struck their breasts and returned to Jerusalem in silence.

QUESTIONS

1. How did the priests and the Jews mock Jesus? 2. What did one of the thieves say? 3. Who stood near the cross? What did Jesus say to His mother? 4. How long did the darkness last? 5. What did Jesus say soon afterwards? What were the last words of Jesus? 6. What happened after Christ had died?

33. Jesus is Pierced With a Spear and Laid in the Sepulcher

TOWARDS evening one of the soldiers took a spear, and pierced the side of Jesus. Immediately

JESUS IS LAID IN THE SEPULCHER

there came forth blood and water.

2. And two rich men took the body of Jesus from the cross, and bound it up in fine linen. They then laid it in a new sepulcher, that had been hewn in the rock. Afterwards they rolled a great stone to the door of the grave. On the next morning the priests and scribes set guards before the sepulcher, and sealed the stone.

QUESTIONS

1. Why did one of the soldiers take a spear? 2. Who took the body of Jesus down from the cross? What did the priests and scribes do next morning?

34. Jesus Rises from the Dead

AS the morning of the third day dawned Jesus rose from the dead, and came forth from the

THE RESURRECTION

grave in all His glory. At the same time there was a great earthquake. An angel of the Lord came down from heaven, rolled away the stone from the sepulcher and sat upon it. His countenance was as lightning, and his garment as white as snow. When the guards saw the angel, they were struck with terror, and fell to the ground as if they were dead.

2. At the same hour some pious women went out to the grave to annoint the body of Jesus. When they came to the sepulcher they saw that it was empty. And the angel said to them: "Ye seek Jesus of Nazareth, who was crucified. He is risen, He is not here. Go, tell all His disciples and Peter."

QUESTIONS

1. When did Jesus rise from the dead? What of the angel? What happened to the guards? 2. Who went to the sepulcher at the same hour? What did the angel say to them?

35. Jesus Appears to His Disciples

ON the evening of the same day the apostles and some other disciples were gathered together in the supper-room at Jerusalem. As they were in fear of the Jews, they had closed the doors. And suddenly Jesus appeared among them, and said to them: "Peace be to you. It is I, fear not." Then the disciples rejoiced to see their Lord and Master.

2. But Jesus spoke again: "Peace be to you. As the Father has sent Me, I also send you." Then breathing upon them He said: "Receive ye the Holy Ghost. Whose sins ye shall forgive, they are forgiven them: and whose sins ye shall retain, they are retained." Then Jesus vanished out of their sight.

QUESTIONS

1. Where were the disciples gathered on the evening of that same day? 2. How did Jesus give them power to forgive sins?

36. Jesus Bestows on Peter the Supreme Pastorship

AFTER His resurrection Jesus remained on earth for forty days. He was often among His apostles, and spoke to them of the kingdom of heaven. He also appeared to other disciples, and on the last occasion, to five hundred of them at a time.

2. One day seven of His disciples went to the lake of Genesareth; Peter, James and John were among them. Suddenly Jesus was with them. He spoke and ate with them.

JESUS BESTOWING THE SUPREME PASTORSHIP ON PETER

3. Then He said to Peter: "Simon, son of John, lovest thou Me more than these?" Peter answered "Lord, Thou knowest that I love Thee." And Jesus said: "Feed My lambs."

4. Jesus asked him again: "Simon, son of John, lovest thou Me? Peter replied: "Lord, Thou knowest that I love Thee." And Jesus said: "Feed My lambs."

5. Jesus spoke a third time: "Simon, son of John, lovest thou Me? Peter was grieved and exclaimed: "Lord, Thou knowest all things: Thou knowest that I love Thee." Then Jesus said to him: "Feed My sheep."

QUESTIONS

1. How long did Jesus remain on earth after His resurrection? 2. Who went to the lake of Genesareth? 3. 4. 5. What did Jesus say to Peter?

37. The Ascension of Jesus Christ

ON the fortieth day Jesus appeared to His eleven apostles for the last time in the cenacle or supper-room at Jerusalem. He ate with them and told them to wait in Jerusalem, until they would receive the Holy Ghost. Afterwards they should preach to the Jews and the heathens. He said: "All power is given Me in heaven and on earth. Go ye, therefore, and teach all nations; baptizing them in the name of the Father, and of the Son, and of the Holy Ghost; teaching them to observe all things whatever I have commanded you; and behold, I am with you all the days, even to the end of the world. He that believes, and is baptized, shall be saved; but he that believes not, shall be condemned."

2. Then He went with His apostles to Mount

THE ASCENSION

Olivet. Here He raised His hands and blessed them. And it came to pass that, whilst He blessed them, He began to ascend, and was raised to heaven. The apostles adored Him and looked after Jesus, until a cloud hid Him from their sight.

3. But as they were looking after Him, two angels appeared to them, and said: "Men of Galilee, why stand ye looking up to heaven? This Jesus, who has been taken up from you into heaven, shall come in like manner, as ye have seen Him go into heaven." The apostles rejoiced at these tidings, and returned to Jerusalem.

QUESTIONS

1. What did Jesus say to His apostles when He appeared to them for the last time? 2. Where did Jesus ascend to Heaven? 3. What did the two angels say to the apostles?

38. Descent of the Holy Ghost

THE apostles went again to the supper-room in which they usually assembled. There they prayed fervently. Mary also, the mother of Jesus, and many disciples were with them, so that they numbered about one hundred and twenty persons.

2. On the tenth day, suddenly, there came a sound from heaven, as of a mighty rushing wind, and it filled the whole house where they were sitting. There appeared to them cloven tongues as of fire, and it came down upon every one of them. And they were filled with the Holy Ghost, and began to speak in divers tongues.

3. Now at the sound of the wind, the people of Jerusalem gathered together. And Peter stood forth, and said: "Jesus is risen from the dead and sits now

THE DESCENT OF THE HOLY GHOST

at the right hand of God, the Father." Many believed and were baptized; and that same day about three thousand were received into the church.

QUESTIONS

1. How many persons were assembled in the supper-room? 2. What happened on the tenth day? 3. What did Peter say to the people?

39. The Church of Christ begins to Spread all over the Earth

PENTECOST being over, the apostles went out into the world, and preached the good tidings of salvation. In the name of Jesus they also wrought many miracles. And the number of those that believed increased from day to day, and the Church

CHRIST GIVES THE KEYS TO PETER

of Christ was established in many lands. The apostles consecrated bishops and ordained priests.

2. The head of the Church was Peter, to whom the Lord had given the supreme pastorship. The successor of St. Peter is the pope in Rome. The successors of the other apostles are the bishops, and the successors of the disciples are the priests.

3. Thus the Holy Catholic Church has existed now for over nineteen hundred years. It is built upon the rock — that is upon Peter and his successors, the popes. It will never cease to exist until the divine founder returns to judge the living and the dead. Happy are they who believe and act as the Catholic Church believes and teaches.

QUESTIONS

1. What did the apostles do after Pentecost? 2. How are the successors of Peter, of the other apostles, and of the disciples called? 3. How long will the Catholic Church last?

ORDER FORM

Quantity Discount

1 copy	$7.00		
5 copies	4.00 each	20.00 total
10 copies	3.50 each	35.00 total
25 copies	3.25 each	81.25 total
50 copies	3.00 each	150.00 total
100 copies	2.75 each	275.00 total

Gentlemen:

Please send me ____________ copies of *Child's Bible History.*

☐ Enclosed is my payment in the amount of ____________ .

☐ Please charge to:

☐ VISA ☐ Mastercard ☐ Discover

My account number is ______________________________

Expiration date: Month ____________ Year ____________

Account name ______________________________________

Signature ____

(Do not send us your card.)

Name ____

Street ____

City ____

State ________________________ Zip _________________

Please include postage and handling according to the following: For orders of $1-10, add $3; $10.01-$25, add $5; $25.01-$50, add $6; $50.01-$75, add $7; $75.01-$150, add $8; $150.01 and up, add $10. Illinois residents add 7% sales tax. All foreign customers please remit in U.S. funds. Overseas customers add 20% of your order total for surface postage. Tel.: 815-226-7777. Fax 815-226-7770.

TAN BOOKS AND PUBLISHERS, INC.
P.O. Box 424, Rockford, Illinois 61105
Toll Free 800-437-5876 • www.tanbooks.com

If you have enjoyed this book, consider making your next selection from among the following . . .